# TELLING ABOUT ME

SHARON J. RICH
ELAINE M. CROCKER
HELEN G. LANGFORD
KATHLEEN ROSBOROUGH

CONSULTANT: TERRY MACKENZIE

The Wright Group®

# Telling about Me

All the children in the illustrations share many similarities, but they are also different from each other. They look different from each other. They like to wear different clothes. They like to eat different foods. And they like to do different things.

You're a special person, too. You have your own family, your own friends, and your own special likes and dislikes.

In your Writer's Notebook, jot down some of the things that tell about who you are. Think about some of the things you would want to tell someone you were about to meet for the first time. What kinds of things about yourself would you tell your best friend? What kinds of things might you want to keep to yourself?

## ALL ABOUT ME

| THINGS I LIKE | THINGS I DON'T LIKE |
|---|---|
| · my home | · shoveling snow |
| · my family | · cleaning my room |

# Introducing ME

## Where I Live

by Peter Cumming with Gary Natar

I live in Igloolik, far north of the Arctic Circle. My name is Gary. My first language is Inuktitut. In the winter, I love to play 🏒 with my friends. I pull my 🛷 across the ❄️❄️ . Most of the time I wear 👢 , a 🧢 , and a 🧥 . But when my dad takes me hunting, my 🧥 keeps me warm. We pull our big 🛷 with a 🛷 or 🐕 .

Sometimes my dad lets me drive the 🐕‍🦺 all by myself. The ☀️ doesn't shine very much in winter. For one whole month there's no ☀️ at all. It's dark even in the daytime when I go to 🏠 .

My best subject is  .

On Saturday night I like to watch 🏒 on 📺 . My favorite team is the 👕 .

In summer, I play 🏏 with my friends. I ride my 🚲 and I like to swim in the 🛁 . I can play late at night because the ☀️ shines all day and night. Last summer my family went on a fishing trip. We lived in a ⛺ . I caught 48 🐟 . My sisters and I went looking for wild 🦆 eggs, too.

My mom works on a 💻 and my dad is the 🔥 chief.

TITLE: "Where I Live"

AUTHOR: Peter Cumming and Gary Natar

Gary used pictographs to inform others about himself.
Did you understand what each picture stood for?
Discuss with a partner any that you weren't sure about.
What did you learn about Gary from his writing with pictographs?
For whom do you think Gary might have written this piece with pictographs?

# Writing with Pictographs

You can write an introduction about yourself, too. Like Gary, you might write with pictographs.

Who could you write to? You might like to write "Introducing Me" for a new pen pal, for a classmate, or for somebody who knows nothing about you at all.

Think about what you want this person to know about you. Refer to your jot notes if you wish.

After you have drafted your pictographs, share your writing with a few friends.

# WRITERS' TIPS

- When you read over your writing, can you think of anything you forgot to include?
- Can your friends suggest anything that you have left out?
- Could you include other pictographs?
- Do your friends think that your writing with pictographs truly tells about you?
- Do they have any questions?
- Is it easy to tell what your pictographs mean?

Use your friends' comments and any of your own new ideas to finish your writing with pictographs.

Another kind of pictograph is a Coat of Arms. A country, family, or person might have a Coat of Arms. When Saskatchewan became a province of Canada, it developed this Coat of Arms. The red lion is a traditional royal symbol. The green background represents green fields. Saskatchewan is a number one wheat grower, so there are three wheat sheaves on its Coat of Arms. Can you think of a state that might use a similar Coat of Arms?

You could design your own personal Coat of Arms. Look back over your jot notes to see what facts about yourself you might include. You could use symbols and pictures to tell about yourself. Decide which personal facts and colors would be best for your Coat of Arms.

# THINGS I LIKE (AND THINGS I COULD LIVE WITHOUT)

What are some of your favorite things? Think about things you like to eat, things you like to do, and places you like to visit.

What are some of your least favorite things? Think about why you don't like these things.

If you read the poem and essay on the next few pages, you'll find out about other people's favorite and least favorite things.

10

# If I Were in Charge of the World

JUDITH VIORST

If I were in charge of the world
I'd cancel oatmeal,
Monday mornings,
Allergy shots, and also
Sara Steinberg.

If I were in charge of the world
There'd be brighter night lights,
Healthier hamsters, and
Basketball baskets
forty-eight inches lower.

If I were in charge of the world
You wouldn't have lonely.
You wouldn't have clean.
You wouldn't have bedtimes.
Or "Don't punch your sister."
You wouldn't even have sisters.

If I were in charge of the world

A chocolate sundae with whipped cream and nuts would be a vegetable.

All 007 movies would be G.

And a person who sometimes forgot to brush,

And sometimes forgot to flush,

Would still be allowed to be

In charge of the world.

TITLE: From *If I Were in Charge of the World and Other Worries*
AUTHOR: Judith Viorst

What things would you cancel or change if you were in charge of the world?

# ESSAY by Betty Miles (excerpt from *The Real Me*)

## On Riding a Bicycle

I love my bike.

It is an old one, red, a three-speed racer from Sears. It has a saddle seat, a basket, hand brakes, and a licence plate that says BARBARA NEW YORK that my father bought me when I got the bike two years ago.

The best thing about my bike is that it makes me free. With my bike, I can go anywhere: visit any friend I want, go to the library or to the store. Or, I can just ride without going any particular place. If I wanted to, I could ride all the way across the country on my bike. Of course in reality my parents would not let me, but the idea is true. Some day when I am older I intend to do it, with a friend and a saddle pack.

I love to ride my bike on a cool sunny day with the wind in my face. I like the way hard pushes make the bike spurt uphill, and I love how it feels to let go and swoop downhill. When I am riding my bike, I feel that I am in charge of all my time. If I want to go fast, I go fast. If I want to laze along and look at all the little weeds and weed shadows at the side of the road, I do that.

When you're riding along on a bike and other people come riding toward you, you feel friendly. They smile, you smile back. It's as though

you know something about each other, which you do: you know how good it feels to be riding. People in cars are not always so friendly. Sometimes they come up behind you and honk suddenly and yell out their window at you. This is mean, not just because it scares you but also because you don't feel private and alone any more.

The worst thing that ever happened to me on a bike was when I caught my front tire in a sewer grating. At the time, I didn't know what had happened. I just knew that I was suddenly falling, very slowly, over my handlebars, and then there was this enormous crack and hurt, and I was lying on the street watching my bike turn over in the air and land on top of me. I thought I was probably almost dead. The man from the gas station ran out and helped me sit up and said I could call my mother from his phone, but when I was up I could tell I was OK, except that my head and my arm hurt. So I just sat on the curb and rested and after a while I rode home. When I got home I started to shake, and then I cried and cried and my mother made me lie on the couch all afternoon. I had a big bump on my head and a bruise on my arm that turned blue, then green, then a disgusting yellow.

The best thing with my bike is something that happens nearly every day: I am riding along Washington Street toward my house in the cool afternoon air. The sun is low and the maples are all lit up gold with sunlight. I am watching the sky turn purple on one side of me and orange on the other, and thinking about what there will be for supper. The wheels of my bike make a little crunching sound on the gravel. My legs are tired from pumping. Then I make an easy turn into my street, and coast softly all the way to my house.

I pedal down the driveway past the yellow kitchen light and get off and push my bike into its place in the shed and close the shed door. My legs still feel as though they're working the pedals, and my hands still tingle from holding the hand grips, and I'm hungry, and I'm home.

TITLE: *The Real Me*
AUTHOR: Betty Miles

# INVITATION 2

## MY FAVORITE (OR NOT SO FAVORITE) THINGS

In your Writer's Notebook, list some of your favorite things. Make another list of things that you don't like very much.

Or you could make a list of things that you do well and a list of things that you don't do so well.

EXCELLENT

Awesome

Choose one or two items from your list to write about. Try to tell why you do or don't like those things. Or you could write about why you do some things well and some things not so well.

WOW

Animals have characteristics in just the same way as people do. In a small group, discuss what some animals are like.

Sometimes people are described in terms of animals—as quiet as a mouse, as busy as a bee, or as sly as a fox. What other examples can you think of? Jot them down in your Writer's Notebook.

The following poems talk about (or show) what some people think certain animals are like.

PRO__

as a peacock

## THE LION
**The lion has a golden mane
and under it a clever brain.
He lies around and idly roars
and lets the lioness do the chores.**

– JACK PRELUTSKY –

SLY AS A FOX

19

# Python

by
Heidi Brown
Ramsay Elementary School

thick, long, big, bite, worried, zigzag, scale, slide, forked tongues, swirls, squeezed, sharp teeth, sheds, slithers, shaky, scared

# IF I WERE

by Tahli Ghitter
Huntington Hills Elementary School

If I were a tiger with black and orange stripes,
    I'd growl at my enemies but wouldn't dare to fight.

If I were a beaver with teeth so sharp and fine,
    I'd nibble all the trees down and not leave one behind.

If I were a cougar with jumping skills so great,
    I'd roam the forest every day and break down every gate.

20

If I were a blue jay with pretty feathers blue,
    I'd fly the skies every second and teach my babies, too.

If I were a kitty cat with sharp nails clipped,
    I'd scratch all the scratching posts and wouldn't leave a bit.

If I were a skunk with a white stripe down my back,
    I'd spray everybody; I'd spray them if attacked.

If I were an elephant with skin so rough and tough,
    I'd stomp on every ant I see; then there would not be one left.

In this story, a lion, Lafcadio, was taken from his natural home, the jungle, and brought to the city. This tale shows how Lafcadio acted when people tried to "civilize" him.

(excerpt from)

# Lafcadio: The Lion Who Shot Back

By Shel Silverstein

But after a while of course he would sign only one autograph at a time with his right front paw because that was more like a man and less like a lion and Lafcadio was becoming more and more like a man all the time. For instance, he stood on his back paws and he learned to sit at the table with his left hand in his lap and his elbows off the table.

And he stopped eating menus.

And he learned to wear dark suits and white shirts with button-down collars and tweedy brown suits with plaid shirts and turned-up collars.

And he learned to wear collars with starch in them.

And then he learned to wear collars with *no* starch in them.

And he kept his tail curled up and seldom let it hang down except when he forgot himself or he had a little too much buttermilk to drink.

TITLE: *Lafcadio: The Lion Who Shot Back*
AUTHOR: Shel Silverstein

23

INVITATION 3

## WHAT ANIMAL WOULD I BE?

Are you like any of the animals on these pages?
If so, which animal are you most like?

Think about an animal you are like. Write
about why you are like the animal you have
chosen. Tell about specific times when you
behaved like that animal.

MOOSE

Share your work with a partner. Does your partner think that you are like the animal you chose? Can your partner suggest other ways you are like the animal you chose? What other animal does your partner think you are like?

# Dear Diary

So far in this book, you have been writing to inform other people about you. A diary is a personal place where you tell yourself about you! A diary helps you remember things that are happening. You can describe daily events in your diary. You can record your feelings and problems in a diary.

In the novel *Dear Mr. Henshaw* by Beverly Cleary, Leigh has decided to start keeping a diary. He addresses his "pretend letters" to the author who has encouraged him to start keeping a diary. Leigh records his thoughts and feelings (especially those he can't share with others) in these two entries.

December 13

Dear Mr. Henshaw,
I bought a composition book like you said. It is yellow with a spiral binding. On the front I printed
 Diary of Leigh Marcus Botts
 Private — Keep Out
 This Means You !!!
When I started to write in it, I didn't know how to begin. I felt as if I should write, "Dear Composition Book," but that sounds dumb. So does "Dear Piece of Paper." The first page still looks the way I feel. Blank. I don't think I can keep a diary. I don't want to be a nuisance to you, but I wish you could tell me how. I am stuck.

Puzzled reader,
Leigh Botts

Saturday, December 23

Dear Mr. Pretend Henshaw,

This is the first day of Christmas vacation.
Still no package from Dad. I thought maybe he
was bringing me a present instead of mailing it,
so I asked Mom if she thought he might come
to see us for Christmas.
She said, " We're divorced. Remember?"
I remember all right. I remember all the time.

Diary of Leigh
Marcus Botts
Private—Keep Out
This Means You!!!

TITLE: *Dear Mr. Henshaw*

AUTHOR: Beverly Cleary

Some diaries tell about special events by describing them and including feelings about the events. Tasha Riley kept a travel diary when she went to England to visit her grandparents.

### January 12

We just got onto the plane and am I ever excited. My dad said that the trip would be a long one, but right now everything is happening fast.

I wonder what my friends at school are doing. Mrs. Davies said to write about the trip to tell the class. I'll draw a picture of the plane to help show them how big it is.

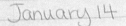

## January 14

Grandma and Grandpa live in a tiny house not far from the school in Liverpool. Their yard is so tiny. Our dog would not be able to run and play there. The houses are all together and not very big. Dad said they are called council houses. I think they are like town houses. Jalke would really like the taxis. They have a funny little seat at the back. I am going to take a Taxi whenever I can.

## January 15

We went to the Tower of London. The armor was neat. Henry the Eighth had the best costume. My sister liked the crown jewels. I liked the knights.

Do you keep a diary? Do you know of anyone who does?

## KEEPING A DIARY

If you haven't already started keeping a diary, you could begin one today. Use a special notebook for your diary entries. You might like to use your diary to record your own feelings. Or you might like to write about the events of today's world so a child a hundred years from now will know what it was like. How else could you use your diary?

*imagine that*

...you had been living a hundred years ago. What kinds of things would you have written about in your diary?

**REVISITING**

Which ways of writing told you the most about yourself? Which ways of writing gave you new ideas about yourself? What were they? Which ways of writing were easiest for you? Which ways of writing did you find the most interesting?

If you decide to publish some of your writing, don't forget to check "Becoming a Writer" for tips on polishing your writing. Also, look back at the Writers' Tips in *Telling About Me.*